D1571141

THE DANCE OF
NO HARD FEELINGS

DATE DUE

Demco, Inc. 38-293

THE DANCE OF NO HARD FEELINGS

Mark Bibbins

Copper Canyon Press
Port Townsend, Washington

Printed in the United States of America

Cover art: Kristen Wright, "Masopust," 2006. Fine art giclée, 24 x 36 inches.

Copper Canyon Press is in residence at Fort Worden State Park in Port Townsend, Washington, under the auspices of Centrum. Centrum is a gathering place for artists and creative thinkers from around the world, students of all ages and backgrounds, and audiences seeking extraordinary cultural enrichment.

LIBRARY OF CONGRESS CATALOGING-IN-PUBLICATION DATA
Bibbins, Mark.
  The dance of no hard feelings / Mark Bibbins.
     p. cm.
  ISBN 978-1-55659-292-8 (pbk. : alk. paper)
  I. Title.

  PS3602.I23D36 2009
  811′.6—DC22

                              2009013346

98765432 first printing

COPPER CANYON PRESS
Post Office Box 271
Port Townsend, Washington 98368
www.coppercanyonpress.org

Abundant thanks to the editors of the following:

The Agriculture Reader, Barrow Street, The Best American Poetry 2009, Beyond the Valley of the Contemporary Poets, Black Clock, Black Warrior Review, Bloom, Boston Review, The Canary, Colorado Review, Columbia Poetry Review, Court Green, EOAGH, fou, Gulf Coast, Interval(le)s, jubilat, La Petite Zine, The Laurel Review, LIT, MiPOesias, New England Review, New York Quarterly, The Paris Review, Red China, Samsara Quarterly, Satellite Convulsions, Stanza (Netherlands, trans. A.T. van 't Hof), *Tin House, the tiny, Under the Rock Umbrella,* and the Underwood Poetry Series broadsides.

Also to Erin Belieu and Mary Jo Bang, always.

to Brian

Contents

3   Bring Us a Souvenir from the Next War

4   There Is No You Are Everywhere

5   Ending in an Abandoned Month

7   We, The Reader

8   Brightening Elsewhere

9   Horoscopes without Telescopes

11   Arriving in Your New Country

12   Echolocation

13   The stars of our favorite shows are all in love but not with us.

15   Blindside

16   Here a Narrative, There a Narrative, Everywhere a Narrative Narrative

19   Forcefield [HAZARD]

32   Redemption

34   Bad Science

35   Dilemma

36   Prophylaxis

37   Redshift

40   Wherewithout

41   I Used to Have the Shampoo

42   Viva Isabella Blow

44   Microburst

45   And Does This Team Look Tasty in Attack

46   Prequel: West Broadway

48   Give Us the Dark That Keeps the Darkness Out

49   Intimacy Keeps Happening Here

50   An Opiate Coating of Disregard Prevails

52   A Perfect Day

53   When They Are Dying They Don't Know
What to Do

55   Forcefield [ARDOR]

67   What Day Is It the Devil Pisses on the Blackberries?

69   Concerning the Land to the South of Our Neighbors
to the North

72   And Further, More

74   Conifers

75   It Buds, It Bends, It Dies in the Glare

76   We are not kissing and the river

77   Analogue

78   Every Nowhere Needs One

79   Sweetlips and Spangled Emperors

80   Little Aggressive Carnivore

81   Why don't we split open

83   Lovelier Near the End

85   Suicides of the '90s,

86   The Devil You Don't

97   *About the Author*

THE DANCE OF
NO HARD FEELINGS

Bring Us a Souvenir from the Next War

In Antwerp this afternoon the Museum of Anaesthesia,
the reason one goes to Antwerp, is closed. A way

to translate nowhere into nothing and the inhalation
thereof becomes a boon, a freak rush around the sun.

The diagnosis is cracked emphasis but the prognosis
is a coming together, niceness, and considerable

kissing in the neighborhoods. We still can't know
anyone but we have a way of not minding not knowing,

and you must be glad the numbness rising in your legs
isn't reading on your face. Europe looks huge

but we've done bigger. Each day people in restaurants
order the wrong things. On the wooden door you see

a small gold sign.

There Is No You Are Everywhere

I'm not sure how it got this early or why we needed
to keep the evening in what we would much later
agree was motion. What could grow so marvelous

and where might I've met you—only endless want
lay ahead, but we figured we'd earned it. Desire our
birthright, rebate checks clog the mailbox and spill

onto the lobby floor—account for them when
you get home; now run naked at the gulls
all you like, I'm waiting for August right here.

Whatever you say sounds better with your thigh
against mine and caught in the camera-phones
of our undoing. Yes you told me what I need

but Brooklyn's awfully far to go for something
you don't even believe; what's miraculous is that
we ever managed to be specific. What's tedious:

insufficiently scandalous secrets. We dig up fire
from nearly anywhere but you're too burnt to burn
or admit we wanted to try what feels almost new.

Ending in an Abandoned Month

Of the citizenry but not exemplary,
another false copy of me returns
to cheap structures that poke
        into the clouds.

        Nauseated, we watch
a two-foot tornado stagger black
up our street, hear the sick smash
of windows hit by giant hailstones.

Every time the world
             ends this way,
I want to thank whoever had
a choice. Perhaps we should have

seen it coming—white kids giving
mad props to zombies, Jersey studs
with waxed eyebrows and brilliant
    buffed nails.   Should I specify

      that here I am with you,
the air a shade somewhere left
of flesh and right of slate, smeared
over our Manhattan as the snow

comes to blunt everything tonight?
Certainly there are too many
    species of weather,
        which is why they're

being replaced by color-coded models
of pure dread. When it's finally over,
years from now, when the storm ends,
              let whoever digs us

out find this headline—SHOOTING VICTIM
        APOLOGIZES TO VICE PRESIDENT—
so they can get a sense of how
        we did it when we died.

We, The Reader

Murder is also singular, no flight inside. So much
rust on rust, the rest of the city secular and slow

as violets arrive—an accident, an argument in birdsong
suddenly ripe. Thrown shadows tell entire buildings:

who's within, time and the density it acquires. Show
us how still. Chords come; we administer letters

to push them down. Propeller or crutch, how
do we get there, to where

we can answer what the jingle is asking.
Make enemies irresistible and rearrange

the heart's holes as someone rolls
a perfect joint in a dark driveway and asks

whether you might go either way.
A thunderstorm comes for three days, three

days of wet fists, but you stay to make
sure what you heard is not untrue. You look

wonderful, what are you doing here with him?
Run away, we, the reader, insist.   Run.

Brightening Elsewhere

They've hired skywriters
to compose clouds in a sky
off-color but clear; such
clever hats the chimneys

wear, so furiously they twirl.
                    Make that
face again and we'll perfect
the picture. Really. Make

that face. Figure and gesture
refuse to engage: there's only so
much one can do.
                    Once I held a couplet

close—too close, in fact; it died—
this and other minor matters
refuse to disappear. An expat
I've become, except I am still here.

Horoscopes without Telescopes

It could feel good to stare at numbers
all day, another job but I can't name any;
still, on a scale of dismal to dazzling,

we should at least aim for a bit of all right—
just keep your examples to yourself
or we can't remove them. If you wind

up with a window and sun I'll get you
something that never dies; it's part
of this conversation we're conceiving—

no initials, only terminals, where nobody
looks until they need to. How many out-
sized '50s-cartoon kisses popped up there,

not the ones the papers are buzzing about
and never on a dare. There was a dictionary
on my lap and a word you wanted but

it was too much. If we're lucky we will
find shame and collaborations and even
more fruitful collaborations and lack

of discretion and dead lobsters strewn
across fields to make the crops grow.
One thing usually true about history,

it's embarrassing. And by which I mean
I've written another letter to you in my sleep
about the time I almost managed to swim,

fully clothed, across the blacked-out bay. I want
it lush all around and so long as bigger trees
make me dizzy, I will find you but not today.

Arriving in Your New Country

Wrong decisions are harder to make than most
people realize, tears flying sideways in a gale.

We swerve in the road so as not to hit dead things,

but I used to know someone who did the opposite.
He liked to drive through them. Stars are most

serious when seen from the back of a pickup truck

while very very drunk, and if someone kisses you
there it doesn't count. I would grab your sadness

as a movie monster would, bring it to the harshest

part of the mountain: I haven't seen this place yet
but I am told weeping is not part of its economy

and everything there is delicious if eaten alone.

Echolocation

The malcontent's lament expands,
expands to symphony as he endures
the bland assault of the anchordork—

he of the cursed hair and carny grin.
Just once, someone on the rack might
stop and ask, *How is this journalism?*

Our navigation: shite. We envy bats
their means by which to locate bugs
and keep from crashing into trees.

Reason's got scarce as a union rep
in the abstraction factory, grim
as a potato box in Chinatown, where,

for his signature body-part graffito,
the hype man was paid in hype—
reap whatcha steal, coin of the real

and all—plus the husk of an overdone
canard, recently brooding and exuding
tepid grease behind a studio window.

Tryst, bender, deli dimebag—love,
could you see Apollo dolling up behind
the rooftops, stroking his golden curls?

The stars of our favorite shows are all in love but not with us.

I'm not acting coy, I'm just terrified
of some rhetorical You—full of red-carpet
menace and dead-end agendas. If we lack
credibility we can steal it, just don't say

—*Eject the bland* [too easy]
—*Impeach the emperor* [again]
—*Where's the remote* [too late]
—*Love me back* [so filled with useless

need, it burns holes in the rug]. Dial up
the days when some enfant terrible could
find himself place-carded next to an uptown
matron, lean over and whisper to her

an obscenity so accurate that she has no
choice but to be fascinated, delighted, etc.
Bring back Charles Nelson Reilly, bring back
Paul Lynde—man, those guys were *gay*—

to show us how it's done. CNN, I'm sick
of your shit, trying to sell me Monsanto
and Boeing. Fox, you can't have it both ways
forever—secrets are insults when everyone

knows them. Don't second-guess elephants'
reactions to caches of elephant bones—
they know better than you, and respect,
as you play it, is frosting on a tar-and-feather

cake. Even with the tease of syndication, our
bloodshot lifestyle can never compete with his,
or hers again, or yours—at least at last I can
measure you—now come, come put me out.

Blindside

We broke into subjects left
alone, piled upon a red neglect
[were moved]. We stuck our
hands into three years of nothing
and pulled out more or less
the same. Dear unreliable lyre,
we stayed strung along and fingered
[all the better to lose you with,
my clear Caribbean sky]. But how
it burned and how we wanted
further trees and how the moon grew
ludicrous pink and how dramatic
the rays and how they eluded
you and how a sentence messed
with us and how the currency
seduced me and how we stole
down to the lagoon and swam
and swam until we were gone.

Here a Narrative, There a Narrative, Everywhere a Narrative Narrative

okay trouble   now a test   when
suddenly everyone begins to grin
      at you   what do you do

      [has been forever grinning]

everyone constantly eats crickets

      what Mexican market   can you not find
    your way out of
      [cricket cricket]

how are you dizzy in the stalls
    who aims the pistol at his son
      who cuts patterns in vellum
        who built the wall around the lake

okay junior exec   mugged in the capital
when you were kidnapped and rolled
    did you think   this is not the man
      I should die with

      [or did you think]

I want him to kiss me and another way of saying so

      [he left a spark on my lip]

    the taxi that took him away
      was a gold spear

[he ran a spear through my lip]

a thousand candles   had sunk
    to the bottom of a lake

        were cast by the kidnappers
            cast from a single mold   and held there

            [looking for looking for looking for you]

one singer   two speakers   four ears   more crickets

      the drum machine

        the need

        to be made   not right

Forcefield

[HAZARD]

Public silence indeed is nothing

—George Oppen

[all night]

we listen

as it claws at the roof

[all day]

we inch
away from windows

the bones

come falling
down the chimney

the bones   are still wet

thanks for the glass dark

for the ropes

    effort

      wine

for letting us kick
and stroke ourself

for the melting metal

thanks
 for the ripped-through

        nothing

         thanks

got legless

        got lost

on red mountains

      the wreckage

the way
wrecked things move

when a wind moves them

find nothing in this
          water

[linger   linger   leave]

a hail of dead men

fills the great net

we wanted but to rectify

this teeming transit

              so an arm

              so I held it

though the face had flown

here lies our music
protruding

from a lakebed

                it swoons

                but silently

and bleeds

[crawl to

                      an end

                  an edge]

        defer suffering

without proof

mercury

in a dirty hat

we see
ourself

but aren't curious per se

if the air ignites

let your king explain

these toppled trees

bird in the engine

poison wings

clouds obscure another   [nearer]   sun

gravity left us

in what had been home

gravity took out our eyes

[thumb]

beautiful visible letters

[sideways]

lights emerged from the pool

swallowed us

[neck]

the remains were scattered

mostly

the rest were eaten

from here the fjords

wrinkle together

everyone wants to roll down

the sides

blissful   we hand away

our teeth

[how we let ourself plunge

and

plunge]

when what we have ruined
returns

its after will harden

to webs of bone

nothing
will grow here

we won't repent

will ruin ourself again

                    because
          the wrongest   rain

    can still
  persist

                inside
                such

constant constant winds

[what if   within them too]
     our skin could turn to song

                and sing us through

Redemption

Here's another rack on which to hang
your critical coat: a flight over the plain

states keeps going and no one notices, the ride
is so smooth; even the inevitable drop

into the Pacific is of no more moment
than the twitch of a sleeping cat's ear.

There's a pack of kids on a nearby
aircraft carrier, talking about

kicking the crap out of someone,
though all I keep hearing is,

> *I can't* [activity] *with you when I'm* [adjective].
> "He likes it that there is no chance to misunderstand pansies."
> —G. Stein

That was ages ago, when everyone's predilections
could spread unchecked and without consequence.

We flourished, all dirty and dazzling
as tranny hookers under the Manhattan Bridge.

> *Yes, but can you* [activity] *when you're not* [adjective]?
> *What if you were slightly* [adjective]?

Today, in the great corporate slideshow
of the heart, the bullet points are blanks.

Today, though I am feeling positively artisanal,
I'm letting you do the work, like you

like to: I'm letting you pretend you're still
the sun, drawing an infernal line through every thing.

Bad Science

A woman at work shed her regional accent and claimed
    to know how to crack

the codes of would-be suitors' answering machines.
    Remember when they couldn't

find us? Six-month passes to the Japanese ramen museum
    and theme park are ¥1,500,

and one must venture—not bad science, just inconvenient—
    all the way to Yokohama,

where there also lives an epic Ferris wheel that doubles
    as a clock. Danger:

you have been singled out for some saccharine
    desperation: ever more

danger. The Italian matriarch mumbles about molecules
    on her cooking show

and compounds we can't imagine strengthen our hair
    while being represented

by sleekly animated constellations—somewhere
    in this digital sky,

lipids are parts of speech and more than myth. For every
    action there is marketing;

in every chemistry set a volcano draws another
    virgin to its lips.

Dilemma

We were swept up into a grubby psychedelia
that mostly made us feel old but nobody cares

what you do when you're fifteen, not really.
I'm pretty sure that was the shortest

year of my life, though I lack perspective,
like a Welsh vampire. Whether this is a by-

product of being undead or from Wales
is tough for me to say—the country has more

segments than even an orange, so how can
anyone know. Also I did the most ludicrous

things to my hair, and these acts will surely
return to bite me somewhere proverbial

during the primaries. Can anyone tell me
how to stop this? My campaign manager

gave me perhaps the best advice,
which is not to try, don't even try.

Prophylaxis

Inflict on foragers a residue
of pain [improbable tinge],

some scar that will not read
in subsequent snapshots of same.

Address the complications
of white leaves hanging from

wires, sticking in teeth.
[If a toucan fell from

a toucan tree and the fruit
of a star fell into the sea,

certain traumas would swell;
prepare to be done to, stranger,

inside our collective malaise.]
Can you recognize the dying

creatures in the lake, the velocity
of something vile increasing,

thriving on the toxins thrown?
Swim in a bucket of know-how,

drink up a river of doom, gather
a smack of missing moons

and keep them for when
your light has run away.

Redshift

You made me want blood then
handed me the blade, now

I have only dragging
steel over everything or fitting

my knees in my mouth, where
I go when I want something

pure or approximately so.
A long blank space will do

or a remnant of blood.
The light arrives

in honeycombs and the wind
through funnels follows

and we are not here
speaking, just crammed.

This can't equal the music
I heard—the interface only

allows a wind of blades
glitched out and aimed

at everything skin. I can't
get near a bloody Mary, its

lewdness, its red forecast
of vomit, though there's solace

in the marketer's
commitment to the many

pills he shills. I feel I haven't
really lost the blood

from my stomach so long
as I can see it on the deck.

The whales are below,
about to unleash

a net of bubbles that will
drive tons of panicky

mackerel to the surface
and to their deaths.

Hunger made us, they'd say,
that's all, as it does you.

The lewdness of the great inflated
bellows of their mouths

is mitigated by the fish, explosions
of blades cutting the foam

with their dying, the gulls
screaming into the blades.

The lewdness
of the pen in my bag,

impaling the banana I got
on the flight from Denver,

the lewdness.
The body is a foe.

Wherewithout

I'm sunk within
a blank; you're tanking,

temperamental, though
everything peeled reveals

a tottering joy. Dollop
of no more, upping

the anterior: we're off
to the theoretical zoo.

Ever have I loved
our alibi—miscreants

hear it and swoon. The pen
tip hides in a Lucite night

as its pigment skitters
and rips up the day.

I Used to Have the Shampoo

with D.A. Powell

I used to have the shampoo
by the balls but the wind hurt my hair so.

I can't get over that retarded girl on the trike,
can't find the apes in the apiary,

can't get hard for the hardtack
and the cannery is closed.

Well, this is just a trumped-up way of saying
your haircut is among the finest in Wyoming.

From the brightly arranged parlors of San Francisco
to the uncompromising river, beside which, huskily, we sang,

you can modify an adverb with an adverb—they do it all the time
        in France—
but I have not left my room in thirty years.

My life is shrinking like a desiccated organ,
wilted japonicas drenched in wine.

Viva Isabella Blow

Tonight we walk through
the golf course where only
an hour ago fog blocked

a moon so brilliant that
we now could cut each
other's hair by its light.

Art on the walls, salt
in the pond, the greenest
grass between our toes—

we asked the driver to stop
at the beach and then
at the carnival and

we woke in Murray Hill
by midnight. Those lives
were probably someone

else's, but it pleased us
to pose alongside them.
Fake it till you break it was

the refrain that propped
us up that summer. *I don't
want to be kissed*

by all and sundry.
I want to be kissed
by the people I love.

Strangers, we knew
better. This will be
a year without hats.

Microburst

Sweet little blondie, I watched you fly, suspended from wires, across the stage.
Shore up, towhead, night is mostly green underneath and you won't mind it.

[a great collision in the wings]
[tempest in a teabag]

What is worthwhile, notorious platinum phony, in your box?

[reek of marigolds]

The actors are the talent—yes, an elastic mass of it—
but even they don't see Eiffel's baby burning.

[on fire] [on fucking fire]
[at night]

Oh and blondie, you sang so loudly. Not sweet   you sang.
[not so sweet at all]

And Does This Team Look Tasty in Attack

Arms and legs cutting
the numbered field

are meteorological
but faster, a flock.

So far I've made
a decent living proving

negatives: warily
I wait, choosing

the nest over
the eggs, acolyte

of mysterious ears
and weirder eyes.

Yes, but what
of exemplary movements

forming arcs and angles
that argue against

the physical, even
as they prove it—

this is what or these are
all we need? Add more

weather to our misery
and I think I trust it is.

Prequel: West Broadway

An actual naked human stands
on a pedestal in the street, naked
and with arms outstretched, naked

among literal feathers blown—
some clinging to skin and hair,
some wavering along the concrete

or skyward—by a fan operated by
an intern. Hair, makeup, lighting all
represented; pedestal, body, feathers

all white. You see this naked body,
this man or this woman, you notice it
but don't stop because you figure

it's only art, in which you don't
believe unless it's used in advertising,
in which you do. There is a war a few

blocks over, another war hiding
behind a melancholy water tower.
Maybe someone will take a hatchet

to our hyphenated necks but we're
not going to bother with bodies
like those anymore. White galleries

up and down side streets hide all the art.
City is hyperbole as ocean is hyperbole
as desert is definitely hyperbole,

oasis burning out on the overrated
horizon where every blue gets
bleached into naked naked white.

Give Us the Dark That Keeps the Darkness Out

We finally *get* the terrain—its fever greens
and where've-you-been-all-my-life browns—
also cars, bridges, likewise decked out.
Admit we bow to a number of things, among
them October, distance to icecaps, radii
of moons. Neglect arrows through but certain
zeros will not rake us in. Obliterate as you
bloviate, bossman, on your occidental rug.
What spectacular thing could you make out
of all you've thrown away, then what would
you devise to make it explode? The proper suit's
a posture, the wrong not yours but occupy some
semblance of a self. Catapult the propaganda,
dip it in disease and hurl it at the fourth
estate. Give back the hook stuck in skin,
the lake-like cold; follow prongs of fire
across denuded plains until we ghost
and summer underground.

Intimacy Keeps Happening Here

There's a ton of the twist
but we're fresh out of shout.

—James Murphy

Squeeze a megalopolis onto an isthmus and look
at what the ocean takes from our buildings; come

back, tomorrow it will seem the same. Marigolds

grow vulgar in every square and the populace puts
oily handprints on the huge cardboard sundial

near City Hall. Why does one block smell like poppers

and another, just south, goosedown? Eventually
we learn to walk through anything, all our rhythms

preprogrammed. Show me what doesn't cohere

and I'll show you something we haven't earned
—no oath, no notes, no fingering RECORD—

even sun pummeling through the humid city air

is a dare. Come on, another dirigible is hooking up
with our tallest building. Truly, it never gets old.

An Opiate Coating of Disregard Prevails

Find a skeleton and douse it with paint:
the organs are linear, emancipated,
not missed: appliances scattered on the sidewalk,
they glisten there still.

> [*merciful razor*]
> [*merciful goat*]
> [*merciful hurt light*]

From concoction to conclusion, we lived
in the desert as though we could apprehend it,
extract what was implied. We stole
water and maps, drove up the steepest inclines,
got by on rattler jerky and tarantulas.

> [*merciful hooligan*]
> [*merciful burning*]
> [*merciful no teeth*]

Acting offended is the best offense. When
I grow up I want to be an activist judge.

> [*merciful fluids*]
> [*merciful trampoline*]
> [*merciful poor years*]

As the plane chases its tail across
the tarmac, the pilot announces that once
the ball is back in our court we're going to
run with it as fast as we can. Now, I don't know
from tennis, or football, or flight, for that

matter, but an airsick bag is metaphor, too,
its coy representation of wings.

> [*merciful wanted to*]
> [*merciful perfect*]
> [*merciful merciful ruin*]

A Perfect Day

Finally all the verbs gave up,
agreeing to throw their
weight behind *to be.* Everything

turned fashionably Zen-like, like
a picnic in early autumn.
Of course you say for someone

somewhere there is no autumn so
it is wasted, but be
quiet now. [This is how you try

to hobble everyone and we've had it.]
The others will weigh in soon,
from the watery edges

of their dosages,
from the straight scars
of their days.

It's a perfect time to resent
vegetarians, fuel-efficiency,
and ideas. It's lovely, sitting here,

watching a cruise ship—*Norwegian
Dawn*—slip up the river,
thinking of deceit. How useful.

The geese are turning, miles over
this place, aiming a kind of gray
fire down at our heads.

When They Are Dying They Don't Know What to Do

We pulled a thousand
turtles out

of the pond, the verboten,
the swollen

puddle of emerald gravy—
oh, hello, noblesse oblige,

come to watch us
work; goodbye, the neighbor

who gave us sticky paper
porn. The canvas of tents

we pitched had basement
stains and there was

nothing else to move
us, so I made

you a new verb,
one they won't hear

here. Freight trains dragged
a tar smell through

another summer, inside
of which I lost

my will
to sleep and ventured

out to satirize
the stars. Guilt seems not

contemporary in the way
regret, at its best,

remains. You've seen most
of what you

shouldn't have, now
it's safe to kill

its context. Sketching
is stealing

and kicking
is how we show our love.

Forcefield

[ARDOR]

It is erotic when parts
exceed their scale

—Lyn Hejinian

one air

rife with yes

and one air

round with snow

we have navigated

through feedback

in an inside-out shell

[once we got this close

and found fire]

take the couch

      the stove you've seen

and even touched me somewhere near

I want more city   to kiss you in
   [you say]

     but anything

       to tell

       is gone

ice   javelins our throats

but the machine around us

has already died

you can leave your hand

on the empty

chair between us

your books too

find   no accuracy

no   wet help

for a sweetly tonguing

[construct]   [consort]

make our verb

a white wire

hooked over

some bleeding sound

a noun

when you
        bade me
                taste you

I loved it roughly
    as much as your knees bent

when you walked

    on your hands

how foolish to follow

a fool I still will

mistaken eyes

I didn't notice you

underneath
    a newly minted paramour

you wound up

wired and weird   on your
                    precipice

        then dove

mouth full of progress

mouth full of intractable

   mouth full of swarm

     full of spikes

       we flew   [fly]

         will fly

      should fly   will have flown

       are flying apart

we harbored in the harbor

bayed at the bay

saw by the sea

nothing else we needed

and left ourself there

[no succor

no syntax   no sleep]

one assumption clung
                to us

        as limpet would
        to stone

        [make of a dolphin

                neither stencil nor symbol

        nor prosthesis
for something unsaid]

if evening is the object

if discretion is not and none

hawk

[hawk whose head

is cocked   and crook'd

and turned

and gone]

please what   then

have we undone

What Day Is It the Devil Pisses on the Blackberries?

The lyric You holds another
  fistful of fruits, easy
  to malign as to be keen on,
a transaction integral to the plot

when wider grow the holes
  in the basket swung by those
  you reckoned wanted goods you stole.
      An elaborate system

of containment—some who do it best
          laugh at others' attempts.
    I mean not to trivialize, but once
we experienced it as agoraphobia—

  real work getting out the door—
  and look what lay there: unreadings
and misgivings, certain chamomile
      confessions and a no-legged race.

As someone-as-someone says, *Come
& diminish me, & map my way.*
    Watching the news is like being
kissed by a sock puppet. In our hearings

and tellings we aim to avoid
    the strains of filth that fade but stay—
          no second acts, sure, but apparently
    no first acts, either. The upshot's

that gossip is totally patriotic and *this*
    is when the fruit fails, and anyway
    it's a better anecdote when someone screws
      you all the way over by listening in.

Concerning the Land to the South of Our Neighbors to the North

How does it feel, Hawaii, to be first, for a change?

The state bird of Delaware flies too fast to be identified—
see, it's already over Nebraska, booming a sonic boom.

Comprised of two ovals, Michigan is known as The Infinity State.

Illinois has some imposing adult stores along the railway.

West Virginia was made overseas and brought to us, chunk by chunk, aboard
container ships.

During his final days, Hiram Warren Johnson, governor of California from
1911 to 1917, subsisted on scorpions and grapes.

No one could have foreseen what a handful Utah would become, influenced
as it is by the contrarian zephyrs of New Hampshire, three states away.

Scientists predict that Colorado will soon be an archipelago,
though not in our lifetime, and Florida shall turn dusty
as the Necco Wafers scattered nightly across Massachusetts.

It is the custom in Maryland to honor the stegosaurus on Stegosaurus Day.

Not even the kimchi of Oregon can rival
the kimchi produced in South Dakota.

Knock knock who's there Texas Texas who no just Texas.

Before it was written, my novel was banned in Rhode Island on account of
the unions.

New Jersey, did you know that one of your shoulders was queer?

The night sky over Iowa resembles flannel, the moon a fluctuating stain.

Engorged fleas of Missouri bounce across the land, crushing all in their
        path.

Has anyone seen Tennessee? It was here a minute ago.

Nevada has kind of a shitty homepage, but not
as bad as that of Arkansas, which lists "Deposit to Inmate Bank
        Accounts" as one of its top five online services.

Washington is rich in natural anagrams.

In the deep and frigid caves of Arizona live fish that started
out in Kansas and got lost on their way to the sea.

Wearing boxer-briefs in Oklahoma will net you a $40 fine, while
the penalty for mixed metaphors in Vermont is garroting;
of course, if you're heard saying "You go, girl" in Alaska, that's two
        months' community service.

Minnesota, can we borrow some brown sugar?

Indiana has a tail—Jesus, a tail!

As in Andorra, the main environmental hazard of Pennsylvania is
        avalanches,
while overgrazing has decimated nearly half of Maine.

New York remains, alas, the only state without a capital.

SOUTH CAROLINA SURE LOOKS DELICIOUS appears on every license plate
in North Carolina.

Wisconsin blames its financial woes on shady investment deals involving
        a chain of make-your-own-scrapple emporia.

Trust me, you do not want to get arrested in Georgia.

Nothing else sticks in your teeth like Wyoming's nostalgia.

The limbo, thought by many to have been invented in Louisiana,
can in fact trace its roots to New Mexico.

Existential and Persnickety are small towns in Ohio, and would you
believe the state fish of Montana is the blackspotted cutthroat trout?

…Idaho…

Mississippi means *gesundheit* in Esperanto.

Satellite images of North Dakota look pretty much like you'd expect, and one
can only avoid Virginia for so long.

Speaking of arcane delicacies, Pewee Valley, Kentucky (pop. 1,436), is famous
           for a dish called leather pie.

Well, this is the first I've heard of Alabama.

Connecticut! we're sawing you in half.

And Further, More

The bumblebees headline, windjerked,
blunt—more boredom under

honeysuckle. Twilight
was designed for us to happen

within it, so move me with your motorik,
your jugular mien.

[lone river martin in a tree
or thousands churning

a black borealis over the water—
choose one or choose both]

We come to believe we behaved
appropriately, but what

do we know, we're only
envelopes indicating the very things

we were meant to obscure.
In the Tiergarten I met

you at the appointed bridge,
yet the stream was narrow

enough to step across.
A tattered moth

followed us around
for hours so we named it

Cremation, then changed it
to Blood Escaping My Hands.

Conifers

I grew into a stuffed animal who wanted
only to insert himself into the fossil record,

to test the mettle of a closeted end
of starless January. [You hurtle forward, you grab

someone's waist: it's as all scouts
know.] I was loosed in dormant sumac;

this much someone, someone else retained. When
it burns you move away

is good enough advice. [Move
advice that burns, burn off

perception of selflessness, get the regard
of a thing: deer ending

afternoon against the snow
holding on to trees, crepuscular trees,

with an almost yellow whatsit overhead.]
Here all can be reduced

to twigs lashing cheeks
as the snowmobile crests another white hill.

Let dim and distraction weave into
our scarves, shrink

our boots till we put a hood
to ice at the edge of the stream,

then drink what's seeping up
and hope it's clear.

It Buds, It Bends, It Dies in the Glare

after Kristin Hersh

Never mind math, mind
fire: underneath

and shredding, still does.
What good's fortune meant

to do—an aperture, a slur—
fault what you turn into

upon looking in any wrong
direction. Where did you,

when did you, meager
youthface and no shirt.

Fine to be alone, to fall
in a box of light alone, to take

it with you allover, finding
certain others, therefore, gone.

Limit seen of snowsqualls,
sandstone, snails—none

your fault but find it here—
a hundred blood footprints

on the bathroom tile
and you're never getting out.

We are not kissing and the river

tricks the boat. Even at night,
colors freeze when they would
rather bleed. He likes delay,

he says, the long ascent to sex.
[first his finger to his lips]
He of the somewhere-wadded-up

mainsail, half hard and too tired
[to the knuckle now] to try—
when in doubt he demurs

then dissolves, spooked
as I and twice as strange.
The glass we handed back

and forth sits on the sill:
mouth- and fingerprints
overlap, more reasonable

as a form of mimesis [out now
and glistening] than simple
trajectory—and what about

the bridge, under which
the boat [back in, slowly,
slowly] has slipped, its

chain of lights, distorted
by the edge of the glass,
just now turned on?

Analogue

There is a magic
[as he calls it]
to keeping something
humming humming humming
on the verge of breaking.
Fine. Distortion comes
to a song of us stuck
between floors, and the hatch
opens to let us everywhere.
We pole-vault over the green
tip of Manhattan and continue
unnoticed. It's as much
as I promised, no? A whack
on the counter gets that lid
off the mayonnaise jar. Inside
find some winter, an iceberg
wandering across black water,
a crowd of berries ready to ripen.
Fine, next time I'm up there
I'll visit Tromsø, stay
for a week and get a reputation.
Some people cast lures
from their duvets and pull up
giant works of art, while others
insist that litigation is
the highest form of flattery.
Why shouldn't he let someone
else fuck him to the mixtape
I made? Everything breaks in
this city. Everything runs, runs fine.

Every Nowhere Needs One

So you obtain ten and I retain
two and you conceal
the sullen denouement beneath
your shirt   Our affect

              was illegal on the world
that circled the world and of which
we couldn't see enough   Couldn't
              lengthen stems or bones

     This western air that you misread
reddens faces about to outlast
the myth of improving conditions
              I'm having trouble

acting complicit   feting better
wines that taste nonetheless of piss
       Oh hell   I left out
          an entire hemisphere

and its ridiculous trees   The juice
in its leaking was not erotic
          the juice in its wiping   less so
Bob's for you and bully your uncle

if you can extract a moral
out of some lesser endeavor
              out of going awhile without
out of sticking a sword in the ground

Sweetlips and Spangled Emperors

We lost the change that looking
makes: less juice in the sluice,
more tear in the where. Severed

boy-twin sits up, keeps going, offers
a sacrifice to news crews—
the dirt, the down, the dormant star.

We carved an elegy into a chunk
of soap, spelled another
with bodies on a hillside

until the usual twits came to warm
a hole in our iced-up lake, leaving
us hobbled and cheated of tongue,

where pain yet peaks under orchidy rain.
Quelles jolies, parentheses—we slow,
go slack as the water within.

Little Aggressive Carnivore

What a wonder it could all
collapse; in the desert a drop
of empathy sinks into
a millionth word for shit
said a million times. If you
can do one thing you're not
supposed to do, you'll do all
of what you're not supposed
to do. You have no self-control,
you have no self at all. We
need someone to funnel it by:
he who would not scar
but never mind, would have
brought cataclysm but got
siphoned off instead.

Why don't we split open

the continuum and churn some gratitude,
make like Jesus—he's the king
of the prom under faux fog—
and hope as many suns

are visible from here.
Consider what entity played yenta
to anemone and clownfish,
then guess what kind of prayers

it wants to hear.
Pull the right lever, pull
the left lever and
everything yields

an untraceable trail.
The older hold longer poses
and make escapes later,
learning ever more there.

In your answer I found
[illegible untenable bipedal]
recordings of our accidents,
eroticisms, mailing lists;

I'll cut me off at my neck for you
and that'll be more than l'amour:
that'll be picking up the tab,
delivering the state on a plate.

What's the use of synths when
peril can't reach us here,
deep in the seat of a stone,
under a half-lit light?

Lovelier Near the End

The fate of the inter-
office matchmaker

is forever to be
sitting on press

releases intuiting one
big happy time zone.

Whither the lamplight
and further

the magic beans—
surely the prospectus

will guide us?
He says *my heart*

beats in the sun,
he says *I'm just saying,*

he says *nobody*
just says, he says

the troops are literal
and I'm working

on my skee-ball game,
he says *we serve*

at the pleasure of
harm's way, he says

Muzak has gotten
really sophisticated,

he also says poison
is happening

everywhere and will
outrun us all.

Suicides of the '90s,

you don't need me to tell you we needed you
and you were not nothing to us. Mimicking into stupor was a better
guess at how to play ourselves—even I was on TV so I shouldn't have
to recount that either. We tried to say heathen but our mouths ended
up spouting a music better suited to driving through a star-tarted
desert. Creepy cowboy got an era, crossword lothario got years, but
what do we call *this* shit? Might makes maybe, to put it mildly.
Branches of science we haven't invented or gotten around to sup-
pressing would alter the hideous tides, keep us from killing what
keeps us alive. The whole world, to the extent that we can name such
an invention, we have sliced open—I never did make it to physics
class but with luck it's not too late, the last so slow to leave so leave
on all the lights.

The Devil You Don't

He started out as just
a wayward scrap of light

and now consumes
whatever he chooses,
cutting a stolen strain

of lyrical ease with his own.
His heart

rolls into the palm of his hand
and waits there like a blister

in a tree.

▲

The faint alluring radiance

that twitches
over the black seafloor,
held up
by a fish made of teeth

and to which are drawn smaller things—
this is how he tries to love.

Were he to put flesh
on you, it would be flame.

Were he to pick you up
then drop you, all through

    the burning sky would you fall.
    And burning still you would rip
           a hole in the sea, the boiling sea.

        ▲

    He turns angels
into the same fire that melts
the guts of the earth

or spews unbearably out of stars,
then makes of their wings endless

    chains from which to swing.
      When the planet's fontanel yields

to his fingerings, he rides, rides,
      covers his ears against
      a rumor he cannot bear.

      His aliases crackle
  over the airport speakers,

  but they are nowhere
and are never going home.

      ▲

Not for a moment
          does he wish for
us to give up our gods. *Renounce,*

he says and shrugs, *renounce and still*
you die and nothing else. But no one

is listening—the poor have stopped,
          the rest likely never began.

          ▲

Here's the best way to see a thing: catch
          the edge of light
                    that burns

          around its opposite, that
                    which it would otherwise
          obscure. If we could view

this light entire, we would call it
god—but then, if we saw collected

               in one place
               all the ants or all
               the abandoned cars or all the dust

               in the world, we would surely
               make that thing god instead.

          ▲

I am going to pull the music
from your mouth and furthermore

I'll take the orange aching light that splits
          your ribs when I or any
beautiful things come at you.

                    ▲

He rolls by on a skateboard, chased by
 snakes of smoke. Helicopters rear

and waver all around him, gusting
                 down the avenue,
        toward the fissured monuments,
           kicking up a blast
of helices that settle like pollen

              in a glittering layer
  over everyone. He adores
    the show, the high

tech of it, the low—but don't broach
              evil, don't bore him so.
                  Clearly this is no Saint

Paddy's Day parade, and he's neither
headed off to some seminar

              nor giving you the eye.

▴

He's going to stick
to the roof
of someone's mouth—American

palate, quintessential mistrust.

He writes fortunes in clear
lip gloss on a funhouse mirror

as the oracles take down their tents
and their oracular fountains

bubble in the rimy night. One finger
in. *Now say*
what you want
more than anything else.

▴

From serrated streaks of fire
he fashions
a subcutaneous matrix,

sightlines to farther green
vistas. The tributes

of the origamists don't last long, but the sound

     of burning swans

blown down a path to the river
     makes music enough for him.

     ▲

     Kids roll hash into
        their cigarettes and spotlights
     turn the smoke pink
        in the trees. If he'd had

        a childhood, he'd have spent it

     running under sprinklers
to cool his smoldering skin. He made

other arrangements
        and found no need for cruelty
     in his hell-as-metaphor,

     wherein he was more often tempted
than the tempter, watching evolution, each

     new thing. Now admirers call
     him up to say they'd seen him

     on TV and are preparing another

way—such is the devotion
he endures
as everywhere a boiling dew

saturates the buildings till they fall.

▲

Oppenheim's cup and the smell
of static arouse him—what other

distortions has he surmounted,
within what circles

of pleasure has he flexed?
The powers that bore

have flown in from the East,
a locust wave blotting out

the scenery. Their bodies pile up
in black drifts through which

he later slaloms. Plastic flowers
warp in the crematorium,

smother the undertaker
with their fumes.

▲

As he rearranges
       body parts, the sex

grows gigantic, the messiest yet. Take him
           by the tail and see better

   at night. Swiveling armatures, nothing's
      your misdeed; randy boy and roguish,

    looking for a light,
  watch the wind turn
to whips that tangle in the stars,

    his gift to you.

        ▲

He strides through a field of rubies
     as comets trail

from his horns. Astronauts
         mistake the streaks

for a runway somewhere safe—this
    is the version they invent when

   we pull them from the trees
    and send them home.

       ▲

Did the president just say,
"I readjust my horned suit,"
    causing our screens to flush
        and flicker blood?

On American highways, cars hydroplane
                through the acid foam
                that slides from blazing
                angels' flanks. When the press
corps cranes its collective neck
        to get a better view,

        the devil turns water in the glass
under the lectern to steam,

            then absconds with his toy
        piano under one arm
            and a seashell pressed
        to his glowing mouth, leaving

the president who is not the president
        trapped in a red room.

                    ▲

You can pretend I live in a burning box
underground,

    that you'd know me if you saw
                me, but I don't

    and you never do.

His smile is an electric fence
            spitting an amazement
of scarlet flowers into the night.

Hell also has a sky, the world
        being devoured by the sun.

            ▲

            Abominable fancy, slide us across
                    the burning lawns.

        That which doesn't kill us
            is merely waiting;
                it will.

Flattery will get you started, boy.

            Hell is coming.

        Hell is here.

About the Author

Mark Bibbins is the author of *Sky Lounge,* which received a Lambda Literary Award. He teaches in the graduate writing programs at The New School, where he co-founded *LIT* magazine, and Columbia University. His poems have appeared in *Poetry, The Paris Review, Boston Review, Tin House, The Best American Poetry,* and *Legitimate Dangers: American Poets of the New Century.* He was a 2005 New York Foundation for the Arts poetry fellow.

The Chinese character for poetry is made up of two parts: "word" and "temple." It also serves as pressmark for Copper Canyon Press.

Since 1972, Copper Canyon Press has fostered the work of emerging, established, and world-renowned poets for an expanding audience. The Press thrives with the generous patronage of readers, writers, booksellers, librarians, teachers, students, and funders—everyone who shares the belief that poetry is vital to language and living.

Major funding has been provided by:
Anonymous
Beroz Ferrell & The Point, LLC
Lannan Foundation
National Endowment for the Arts
Cynthia Lovelace Sears and Frank Buxton
Washington State Arts Commission

For information and catalogs:
COPPER CANYON PRESS
Post Office Box 271
Port Townsend, Washington 98368
360-385-4925
www.coppercanyonpress.org

The text is set in Minion, designed by Robert Slimbach in 1990 for Adobe Systems. The headings are DIN Mittelschrift, designed by Albert-Jan Pool in 1995 and licensed by FontShop International. Book design and composition by Phil Kovacevich. Printed on archival-quality paper at McNaughton & Gunn, Inc.